Listen to your Parents
by Benjamin Zephaniah

Pearson Education Limited
Edinburgh Gate
Harlow
Essex
CM20 2JE
England
and Associated Companies throughout the World

Listen to your Parents was originally published in 2003 by Aurora Metro Press in the anthology *Theatre Centre: plays for young people*, introduced by Rosamunde Hutt.

This educational edition first published by Pearson Education 2007

Listen to your Parents © Benjamin Zephaniah 2003

The right of Benjamin Zephaniah to be identified as author of this work has been asserted in accordance with the Copyright, Designs and Patents Act 1988.

Activities by Emma Lee

All rights reserved. No part of this publication may be reproduced, stored in a retrieval system, or transmitted in any form or by any means, electronic, mechanical, photocopying, recording, or otherwise without the prior written permission of the Publishers or a licence permitting restricted copying in the United Kingdom issued by the Copyright Licensing Agency, 90 Tottenham Court Road, London, W1P 0LP.

All rights whatsoever in this play are strictly reserved. Application for a licence to present performances including professional, amateur, recitation, lecturing, public reading, broadcasting, television and translation into foreign languages should be applied for, before rehearsals begin, to Peters, Fraser, Dunlop, Drury House, 34-43 Russell St, London, WC2B 5HA.

Cover image © Nick Dolding / Taxi / Getty Images

ISBN: 978-1-4058-5686-7

Printed in Great Britain by Scotprint, Haddington

The Publisher's policy is to use paper manufactured from sustainable forests.

Contents

Characters	v
Scene One	1
Scene Two	4
Scene Three	8
Scene Four	10
Scene Five	14
Scene Six	16
Scene Seven	20
Scene Eight	23
Scene Nine	26
Scene Ten	32
Scene Eleven	34
Scene Twelve	36
Scene Thirteen	39
Scene Fourteen	45
Activities	47

Characters

MARK

WALI

MOM

DAD

VOICES   CHURCH CONGREGATION AND CROWD OF KIDS

The play is set in and around the home of the CAMPBELLS, *a Black British family living in Birmingham. The* CAMPBELL *family consists of* MARK *and his* MOM *and* DAD *– his sister* ANGELA *and baby* CARLTON *need not appear.*

Scene One

MONDAY

MARK *is sitting on his bed looking in his bag.*
WALI *addresses the audience from a platform/pulpit.*

WALI On the first day God created the heavens and the Earth. Then he created flowers and trees, and humans beings and living stuff that creep upon the surface of the Earth. And he looked down upon the Earth and he saw that it was good. Then for some strange reason he created school. And Mark Campbell attended one such school in the great land known as Birmingham. And it was there that Mark Campbell created a great opportunity for himself, and he went for it.

They both break into football terrace style chants.

BOTH Villa *(Clap, Clap, Clap)* Villa *(Clap, Clap, Clap)* Villa *(Clap, Clap, Clap)*

MARK *addresses the audience.*

MARK Yes this is it, I can't wait. I could be playing for Aston Villa. Me, Aston Villa, brilliant innit? And here it is, look at this *(takes shirt out of bag)* – me Aston Villa shirt. I wanted the whole kit but Mom said she couldn't afford it, but the shirt's OK, no it's more than OK, it's wicked guy. I wasn't even doing anything special, just playing around on the pitch after school and I could see this bloke standing there with Mr Collins the P.E. teacher. At first I thought he was a parent or something. Then when we finished playing Mr Collins called me over and I thought, O, O, I'm in trouble again, but I wasn't. The bloke said, 'I've heard a lot about you Mark. What are you doing next Saturday afternoon?'

Scene One

So I said, 'Playing football,' and he said, 'Do you want to go to Villa Park and play some football?' And I said, 'What actually *in* Villa Park?' And he said, 'Yes lad, we're having trials, we're looking for some players for the junior team and you look pretty good to me.' And then I started to tell him that I wasn't even playing me best today and that I usually score about three goals in every game, and that I play even better on a full-size pitch, but he said I should save all me energy for Saturday. (MARK *chants.*) Villa, Villa, Villa.

Music.

MARK *picks up his book and begins to read.*

> Red ripe Mangoes on Lozzell's Road,
> Ackees on Heatfield,
> And Callaloo for all on Witton Road,
> Jamaica must be here somewhere.
>
> There's Reggae in the morning
> Reggae at noon
> And Reggae is played on Soho Road at night
> For grown ups and foxes alike.
> Jamaica must be here somewhere.
>
> Coconuts and cashew nuts cook themselves,
> And the aunties and the uncles
> Walk like they have springs in their feet
> And drums on their minds,
> Is this Jamaica?
>
> Jamaica must be here somewhere,
> I can taste it,
> I can smell it,

Scene One

>Everybody is talking about it,
>There are Jamaican newspapers in the corner shops
>And Jamaican curls in my hair,
>You can't fool me.
>Jamaica must be here somewhere.

Pause.

>I got two of these books, both exactly the same, one for me and one for me Mom. I wrote the poems meself and sellotaped them together. Look, see what it says there? Published by Mark Anthony Campbell – Limited. And there's the title, it's called *Life*.

Lights fade.

Scene Two

In the next room, MOM *and* DAD *are in bed when the baby starts crying.* MOM *goes to comfort baby.*

MOM OK lovely, what's the matter? What is it, your belly? You got wind? Now don't tell me you want milk cause you just had your milk – so what's the matter with my little darling? (*Baby cries even louder.*) Come, come now, what's the matter beautiful? What can I do for you pretty boy, hey?

DAD I wish that baby would shut up. How the hell am I suppose to work if I can't get a good night sleep? I get it in me ear hole every night from that child. How the hell am I suppose to earn money if I can't get a decent night sleep?

MOM What do you want me to do? I mean what do you expect, it's a baby you know, babies cry, that's what they do. Gosh what's wrong with you, you used to complain when Mark used to cry. You used to complain when Angela used to cry, now you've started complaining again, but hey, you never complained when it came to making babies. Oh no, you didn't have any complaints then. In fact you were very keen, too keen if you ask me.

DAD Shut up woman.

MOM Now look at you, you want me to shut up, you want baby to shut up, you want Angela to shut up, and you want Mark to shut up. But why don't you shut up, do you know how to shut up? Because from what I've heard you was the biggest cry-baby in Edgbaston, and from where I'm sitting it looks as if you haven't stop crying yet.

Scene Two

> MARK *addresses the audience as if to distract their attention from his parents' argument.*

MARK Wali Ahmad, he comes to my school, he's me best friend, he thinks I'm a bit weird. He said that I should mek up me mind about what I want to be, a poet or a footballer. I told him I wanna be both, Eric Cantona did, he was a poet and a footballer and his poetry didn't stop him from being a good player, did it? But sometimes I think the rest of his team didn't understand him, they thought he was a bit soft.

> *Sound of baby crying gets louder.*

DAD Shut up, child.

MOM You shouting at him ain't gonna help, is it? Maybe if you tried picking him up and showing him a bit of love, maybe that would help.

DAD Who me?

MOM Yes you, who else?

DAD Stop being lippy and get that baby to shut the hell up, I wanna get some –

MOM (*interrupting*) What do you mean get that baby to shut the hell up? It's a baby just in case you haven't noticed, a living breathing thing, do you think I can get him to stop crying just like that, well if you really think that's the way it is, *you* get him to stop crying.

DAD Getting him to stop crying is not my job woman, it's your job, that ain't a man thing, it's a woman thing, that's your business, now sort it out.

> *Light on* MARK.

MARK (*to audience*) I've lived here all me life, born in Aston, well Dudley Road hospital nearby. Supported Villa all me life. So next Saturday I'm gonna wear me Villa shirt

Scene Two

with pride. Yes guy, I'm gonna big it up, I mean, I don't know any Aston Villa player that's a poet and I don't know any Aston Villa player that's born in Aston, so I'm gonna be different, trust me, the original you know what I mean? True Villa fan, true Villa style.

DAD   You just be careful how you answer me back, you know what I'm saying woman. Don't get me angry now, all I want is a good night sleep, some peace and quiet and a good night's sleep, and if you was a decent mother you would know how to keep your children quiet, and you wouldn't be speaking to me like that.

MOM   And if you was a decent father you would have some more patience with you children, and you would have some respect for your wife, you can't go on like this you know, you go on all religious so don't you know that judgement will come, don't you know that God will find you? You say you're a man, so live like a man.

DAD   Yes and you're a woman so just shut your big mouth and stop answering me back. Remember this, I run tings, right? I control the scene, you must know that no woman will never rule me, I have dominion, and is God give me that, so just rest it.

Light on MARK.

MARK   When I came home from school and told me Mom that I was going for trials she was happy guy, she's cool, but I ain't even told me Dad yet. He didn't give me a chance to say anything – when he came home from work the first thing he did was send me and Angela to bed and start shouting at me Mom and that's all he's been doing all night, shouting. (*sarcastically*) Angela's all asleep, in her little bed, with her little dolls, and her little plaits on her little head. Boy can she sleep. Sometimes she can't even get up in the morning. When she grows up and she's my age she could go for trials because they have girls' teams now, you know, and if I teach her everything I know she'll be good, won't she? I wanna sleep now. It ain't Carlton's fault, is it? He's just a baby.

Click. Lights fade.

MARK Good night.

Scene Three

TUESDAY

W<small>ALI</small> addresses the audience from platform/pulpit.

W<small>ALI</small> On the second day, Mark did forty press-ups, 'cause press-ups help build upper body strength, and upper body strength is needed if you want to be a powerful winger. And on that day, in the land of the Brummie, Mark also done forty squats, twenty jumping jacks, and his knees were brought unto his chest two score and six times, and that was before his cornflakes, not bad hey.

M<small>ARK</small> is playing invisible football in his room.

M<small>ARK</small> Four more days and I'll be there, Villa Park.
And it's Mark Campbell doing a thing,
Yes, it's Mark Campbell on the right wing,
Look at Mark Campbell, he's on a roll,
Here comes Mark Campbell... yes, it's a goal.

Pause.

Hey, you know something, one thing I haven't done yet is write a football poem, well come to think about it, I just did. Sometimes poems just come like that. You can't force poems, you can't just say OK today I will be inspired, inspiration can come at any time. No one knows where inspiration comes from, if I knew where inspiration came from I'd go there wouldn't I? It can come when you're working, or when you're eating, or it could come like it says in the Bible, 'Like a thief in the night.' Well, it doesn't say *inspiration* will come like a thief in the night, it says *the day of the Lord* will. Before I decided that I wanted to be a poet, I thought I

Scene Three

wanted to be like me Dad, a preacher in a church like, but then I changed me mind.

Scene Four

In Church. DAD *is at the pulpit preaching loudly.*

DAD And when we look in the world we see wars and rumours of war, we see spiritual wickedness in high and low places, oh my God. We see a world where people do not know their left from their right and their right from their left because they have been tricked by the ways of the world. Let me hear you say, 'Amen.'

CROWD Amen.

DAD Let me hear you say, Hallelujah.

CROWD Hallelujah.

DAD This is a dirty world.

MEMBERS OF THE CROWD Yes, yes.

DAD This is a wicked world.

MEMBERS OF THE CROWD Tell them brother. Truth.

DAD This is a world where children are having children, this is a world full of greed and envy. This is a world where children have no respect for their elders and this is a world where elders have no respect for God. This is Sodom and Gomorrah.

Big crowd response.

DAD And if we not careful, people, we shall be like Lot's wife, who turn into a pillar of salt, why? Because she looked back. That's why when we leave this world we must not look back, praise God.

Scene Four

CROWD   Praise God. Hallelujah.

DAD   We must not be like the weak woman, unclean and unholy, and we must resist the temptations on the flesh.

Light on MARK.

MARK   (*to audience*) I listen to me Dad and Pastor Bailey and some of the other people preaching in the church, and they're shouting loud and sweating, and banging the tables and stamping their feet and waving the Bible around, and I thought, God man, did Jesus preach like this? I don't think so.

DAD   (*still preaching*) But what is going wrong? We need to analyse the situation and consider what is to be done. We need to ask ourselves, what it is that we need to do, to save ourselves from the brimstone and the fire. Well, my people, the answer is simple, praise the Lord. The truth is that this is not a complex or a difficult thing. We must do two things, Hallelujah. We must let the world know that Christ is not history, Christ is living, Christ is now, and we must put back the Lord Jesus Christ into our lives, we must bring Jesus right into the culture of society. Christ must be the inspiration for all of our politicians, Christ must be the inspiration for all of our teachers, he will lead us out of the darkness, he will lead us into the light, Christ himself must lead the way. Thank God.

CROWD *response.*

DAD   Praise Jesus. And secondly, we must rebuild the family – the family is the rock that holds up society. If you don't have discipline in the family, how can we have discipline in the schools? If you don't have discipline in the family, how can we have discipline in the factories? How, in the name of God, can we have discipline on

Scene Four

the streets, if there is no discipline in the family? God is the father, God is the son, God created families for us because families work best. Let me hear you praise the Lord.

CROWD Praise the Lord.

DAD Let me hear you say, Hallelujah.

CROWD Hallelujah!

Light on MARK.

MARK (*turning to audience*) I reckon Jesus spoke soft and quietly like. I reckon he had manners, you know what I mean? He would say great wise things that would make people be 'Cool', bet he would drop phat lyrics guy, I don't think he'd be shouting his mouth off like a mad man.

DAD We have moved so far away from the word of the Lord, that there are families today where the woman thinks that she is the head of the house, and that she has rights over the man. Some women today will actually say that they want to be independent and they want to be in control. So this is suppose to be liberation, this is suppose to be progress, this is suppose to be the modem world, them call it feminism (*laughs sarcastically*) but I know... and God knows... this is wrongism. (CROWD *laughs.*) This is Satanism. Don't take my word for it; let us go to the Bible for guidance. It is written in the Book of Ephesians Chapter Five. 'Submitting yourselves one to another in the fear of God. Wives, submit yourselves unto your own husband as unto the Lord. For the husband is the head of the wife, even as Christ is the head of the church. Amen.

Pause.

Scene Four

These words are not made up by me, people.

Pause.

But I am saying to you today, we must work towards rebuilding back the family. Men know yourselves, and know your responsibilities, and woman, know that God has said man is the head, so submit yourselves to him, and praise the Lord.

CROWD *goes wild.*

Scene Five

MARK   (*to audience*) The preachers say they want to be like Jesus right? But Jesus preached every day, to loads of people, multitudes of people, so I reckon if Jesus preached so much, so loudly, everyday, he would have some serious throat problems. Check dis –

Surely it is good that football is played by the pure in heart,
For they who lose *not* their tempers may apply their minds wholly unto the brilliant tackle,
And they that are chilled and calm
Shall be known as the chosen few,
They shall be called gifted,
Good guys,
And wicked strikers.
But yea I say unto ye
Those that bully and kick up man shin
Those that kick heels
Shall be burnt by their ill gained salty sweat
And many red cards will be in their midst,
Yea I say unto the spectators upon the terraces,
Those that are arrogant and loud mouthed shall fall upon the unforgiving pitch
And dwell among the worms
And the spit of opposing defenders. (*beat*)

That ain't the Bible or anything, that's just me messing about. But really, think about it, right, if Jesus played football he would have to be the captain because he was a leader of men, and that team would get no red cards. Actually, it would be even better if he was a referee, then he could bring the spirit of the Lord upon all the players before the game and the players would all respect each other – a bit like girls' football.

Scene Five

Pause.

> I just went in the bathroom right, and I could see this towel – it had blood on it. Mom tried to hide it but I could see it. I hope it ain't gonna start up again.

Scene Six

Off-stage, a group of kids are shouting abuse at WALI, *outside school.*

KIDS Asylum creeper.
Can't even speak English.
Your Mom stinks.
You're a scrounger and a thief.
Hey, you look good in the dark.
You need some food aid.
Even your Dad thinks your Mom's ugly.

WALI (*shouting back*) Leave me alone, my English is better than yours. I got higher marks in English than any of you, so you should shut up.

MARK *enters.*

MARK What's up Wali?

WALI It's them lot, they're going on with all that stupidness again.

MARK Don't worry about them.

WALI I don't worry about them, I was born a Brummie, and I'm still a Brummie. I know that at least two of them lot are foreigners. That boy there, him, the one who keeps calling me asylum creeper, he comes from Nottingham. That's miles away. And him the other one, the big one with the mash up nose, he come from London, and he calls me a foreigner? Have you heard the way he talks? They just jealous because I score more goals than them.

MARK Well, I won't call you any names but you can't score more goals than me.

Scene Six

WALI	Yeah, I bet you're wrong, if that man from Aston Villa saw me playing he would pick me before you, he only picked you that day 'cause he didn't see me.
MARK	Yeah, yeah.
WALI	Yeah, you know it. Did you see football on the television on Sunday?
MARK	No, there wasn't any.
WALI	There was… Afghanistan played, and guess what? Afghanistan won. Three one.
MARK	I didn't see that, who did they play?
WALI	I can't remember now, some foreign team.
MARK	See, you don't even know who they played. No offence guy but you gotta face the truth, no one's ever heard of Afghanistan Football Club.
WALI	Just because you haven't that don't mean everyone else hasn't, lots of people know about Afghanistan.
MARK	Listen guy, Afghanistan might have a couple of good cricketers but I bet you can't name one famous Afghan football player.
WALI	I can.
MARK	Go on then.
WALI	Em, em, what's his name now? Em, he's really famous but I can't remember his name now, but he's really good.
MARK	See you can't, and they're suppose to be your favourite team. OK then, how many other Afghanistan supporters are in our school?
WALI	Loads.

Scene Six

Mark Loads?

Wali Yeah loads, there's me, and Anwar, and Hamid.

Mark That's amazing, there may even be four of you, gosh, that's great. I suppose if your parents come from Afghanistan you gonna support them. I supported Jamaica once, only for six weeks. But you gotta admit it, England ain't worried about Afghanistan, Brazil ain't worried about Afghanistan, Afghanistan have never, ever made it to the World Cup, and maybe they never, ever will.

Wali Maybe they just can't be bothered, maybe they don't want to play in the World Cup. Whose world is it anyway?

Mark I'll be in the World Cup before they are, one day I'll be there, you wait.

Wali And you're gonna be the best poet in the world, as well?

Mark Of course guy, but there's no such thing as the best poet. All poets are equal, but right now I'm reading as much poems as I can, and I'm reading loads when I'm not busy with me football. My plan is to write at least one poem every day, maybe more, but at least one.

Wali Come on, what's so good about poetry? Poetry's not that important.

Mark It is guy, poetry's bad. This is the way I see it right, I'm talking to you now, which is a bit like giving a part of meself to you.

Wali Get off, I don't want a part of you.

Scene Six

MARK   Don't be silly, what I mean is I'm communicating with you, right? But then when I write a poem, and I read the poem back to meself, it's like communicating to meself, talking to meself.

WALI   I thought that when you start talking to yourself it means you're going mad.

MARK   Shut up, you know what I mean. Seriously guy, sometimes I say things that even surprise me. They're my poems, I write them, and I still get surprised. It's difficult to explain but poems help me to chill out and make me stronger.

WALI   I thought press-ups make you stronger.

MARK   Wali, stop messing.

WALI   I'm only joking, I know what you mean.

MARK   Anyway a poem a day, that's me ambition. You know what? From now on I think I'm only gonna share me poems with special people like me Mom.

WALI   Special?

MARK   Oh yes, and you of course, if you stop messing about.

Music.

Scene Seven

MARK *in his room.*

MARK Wali's alright, he was born in the same hospital as me. People think he's soft but he ain't. His parents' house got bombed in Afghanistan, and his sister just disappeared, then his Mom and Dad had to walk for hundreds of miles to save their lives and his Mom was pregnant, then when they got here Wali was born. We're lucky in this country guy, at least we don't have to go through all that. (*beat*) That Mrs Macy meks me sick. Today I wanted to show her some of me poems but she doesn't even like poetry. She's getting the class to learn a poem right, and I had me own book of poems in me pocket to show her. So when she came to me, I said to her, 'Do you like poems, Miss?' and she said, 'No, not really Mark, but I have to teach poetry as part of English.' That's terrible innit? Just think if there was a Maths teacher that didn't like numbers, or a P.E. teacher that didn't like games. (*beat*) Check dis. I didn't tell Wali but today I kissed Maria Shah. She said she would give me a kiss if I said a poem for her, so I made up something quickly in me head, nothing important, just a few lines.

I know a wicked girl
She's the best girl in the world,
Her name is Maria and I really love to see her,
And no matter where I see her guy I wanna drop a rhyme,
And when I drop a rhyme I mek her smile every time.
  (*beat*)
She laughed, as she always does, and then she kissed me. She's alright but she tasted of baked beans guy.

Scene Seven

Pause.

Better get some sleep now – school tomorrow.

Click. Lights out.

MARK Good night.

In the darkness, sounds of struggle.

DAD You will do what I say.

MOM I will not.

DAD You will do what I say because without me you'd starve, without me you are nothing. I keep you.

MOM Typical man. Well, I'll get a job and keep myself.

DAD Typical man, I'll give you typical man, if you don't shut it I'll slap ya.

MOM That's you answer to everything ain't it. You have a low intelligence you know, you ain't got much upstairs.

DAD What you saying?

MOM Think about it.

DAD I'm not joking, don't get me mad.

MOM Oh shut up.

Light on MARK.

MARK *(whispering to himself while his parents argue)*
I know a wicked girl
She's the best girl in the world,
Her name is Maria and I really love to see her,
And no matter where I see her guy I wanna drop a rhyme,
And when I drop a rhyme I mek her smile everytime,

Scene Seven

Smile everytime I mek her smile everytime
And when I drop a rhyme I mek her smile everytime.

Lights fade.

Scene Eight

WEDNESDAY
*Lights up. W*ALI *is standing on platform/pulpit.*

W<small>ALI</small> On the third day Mark did fifty press-ups, sixty squats and sixty jumping jacks, and his fitness increaseth greatly. And so it was on that day, in the safety of his own room, far from any Birmingham City supporters, he did forty sit-ups, for sit-ups maketh strong stomach muscles, and strong stomach muscles bringeth forth an awesome six-pack. Then he looked down upon his belly and he saw that it was cool.

W<small>ALI</small> *jumps off the platform and joins* M<small>ARK</small> *on the street, they start kicking a ball around.*

M<small>ARK</small> Let's not go into school guy, let's wag it.

W<small>ALI</small> Shall we?

M<small>ARK</small> Yeah guy, don't worry, let's go to the corner shop and nick some chocolates and crisps and stuff, and then we can spend the whole day practising in the park. Me Mom won't know because she doesn't really check up on me, and I left home at the usual time anyway. I just can't be bothered guy. I don't mind the lessons and that, but I hardly slept last night.

W<small>ALI</small> OK, too much school ain't good, that's what someone told me. But why can't you sleep anyway?

M<small>ARK</small> Nothing. (*He pauses as he thinks about how to ask the question.*) What do you do when your Dad hits your Mom?

W<small>ALI</small> He doesn't hit my Mom.

Scene Eight

MARK What do you mean, have you got one of them back to front family like what they preach about in church, is your Mom a feminist or something?

WALI What are you going on about?

MARK I'm just asking you what happens when your Dad hits your Mom.

WALI And I just told you that he doesn't.

MARK So what happens when your Mom hits your Dad?

WALI Don't be silly, she doesn't hit my Dad. My parents don't hit each other.

MARK You're lucky, guy.

WALI If your parents are fighting you should talk to a teacher in school, or even a copper, because if your Dad's hitting your Mom he could be locked in the nick for it.

MARK Your parents don't fight and they don't even go to church. I tell ya guy, just because you go to church that don't mean you're good, and some good people don't even go to church and they're cool. Your parents don't go to church, do they, hey, do they?

WALI No, well we don't have churches, we have mosques, but it the same thing really. Anyway, no, my parents don't go.

MARK See, they don't go to church, or mosque, and they're cool.

WALI Hey Mark, maybe we should go back to school?

MARK No way, I'm not going there.

WALI Look at them lot over there, so many of them, all wagging it.

Scene Eight

Mark Yeah look at them, they're gonna get caught 'cause they're so noisy, and they're puffin' draw. I know a couple of them, they carry blades.

Wali At least we're not carrying weapons or puffin' weed.

Mark Hey did you know that it was Aston Villa and a couple of other teams that started the first ever football league?

Wali How do you know?

Mark I know guy, I read about it. There's this letter right, it's still around today, and it's from the chairman or something of Aston Villa, to these other teams and it's saying let's get together and start a bit of a league. And most people think that football was invented in England right, but they had a kind of football game in China about four thousand years ago. They never had a proper ball; they just used a pig's bladder or something.

Wali What, a pig's bladder, did they eat it afterwards?

Mark Stop messing. Anyway, the first real ball was made in Mexico right, but it was some English people that made the rules up, and English people made the first proper pitches, so I suppose football is an English game.

Wali I bet the Afghans did it really.

Mark Yeah you would say that. Come on, pass me the ball, I gotta practise all me skills. Keeping the ball up, dribbling, you know, penalties and things like that. Mr Collins the P.E. teacher told me that there's gonna be loads of kids there, from different schools, so I gotta play good.

Music.

Scene Nine

Mark is in his room, reading.

Mark What is the price of a baby?
A baby that will live long
A baby that will shine each day
Come what may.
It need not have a perfect father,
It need not have a perfect mother,
It need not be the son of a prince,
Or the daughter of a chosen one,
All it needs is the sweet smell of love
And a place that is sane and sheltered.
A beautiful smile once told me that
Babies need
But it's not about greed,
And I am so sure that smile would not lie.
So what is the price of a baby?
And do babies get cheaper the less they cry?

Lights change.

The parents' bedroom.

Dad Doris, Doris, Doris, wake up – wake up.

Mom What?

Dad Get me some tea.

Mom What?

Dad Get me a cuppa tea.

Scene Nine

Mom What's the matter? Are you sick or something? Do you know what time it is?

Dad I ain't sick, I just want a cup of tea, yeah. Now hurry up.

Mom Come on, make it yourself. I'm tired man, I've been on me feet all day.

Dad So you tired are you? You've been on your feet all day have you? And what about me? I've been running up and down in that damn warehouse like a madman all day. I'm the bloke that left this house at six-thirty this morning and never returned until seven this evening. I'm the one who's been on their feet all day, me, yeah me, the one who brings the money in this house. Your work ain't nothing compared to what I do. And if I didn't do it you wouldn't have a bed to sleep on.

Mom So what you saying, you don't think I work?

Dad That's right, you don't work, you can't call looking after children work, you're a woman, you're suppose to take these things in your stride. You're built for running the house, now get me cup of tea.

Mom No, I've done my work for today, get it yourself.

Dad I said get me some tea.

Mom No.

Dad I'm gonna tell you one more time, and only one more time, get me some tea.

Mom And I'll tell you one more time, no.

Dad Look at that. What kind of wife are you? I ask you for a cup of tea and look at the way you answer me.

Mom Yes, well look at the way you treat me! I make your breakfast, I prepare your clothes, make your lunch …

Scene Nine

	When you get home I put food on the table, if I can do all that I'm sure you can do a simple thing like make yourself a cup of tea.
Dad	Shut up and get me tea.
Mom	No.
Dad	What?
Mom	No.

He slaps her. Baby cries.

Mom	(*crying*) You see what you've done. Move from me.
Dad	You can't tell me to move, you should know that. (*He slaps her.*)
Mom	Take your hands off me, I can't take it any more man, I'll fight you back.
Dad	You can't fight me you know. I run this house (*slap*) And ain't taking no nonsense from you So just get your arse outta the bed and get me tea. (*slap*) If you got me tea in the first place then every ting would be alright, ain't it? (*slap*) But you, you're a stubborn bitch (*slap*) You are a lazy, lazy slut (*slap*) If I could live my life again, you think I would marry you, Not at all, because you are trash You're Rubbish. You're nothing, you bitch… (*slap*)

Mark, in his room, speaking over the beating to drown it out.

Mark	Wali's Dad took him to the pictures and the car show in the summer holidays. I've never been to the pictures

Scene Nine

                and I'd love to go to a car show. He said there were hundreds of cars, new ones, old ones, cars that had three wheels, cars for the future that shouldn't need any petrol. Wish my Dad would take me.

        Mom *is now losing the fight.*

Mom   Please leave me alone, I really can't take no more of this.

Dad   I don't done with you yet, whore. I gonna teach you some manners. When you talk to me you will talk to me with respect, you see. (*slap*)

                When I say move, you must move, you see.

                You could read a million of those books about woman's rights. (*slap*) In this house I'm the one who is right, you see. (*slap*)

        Mom *is panting – losing breath.*

        Light on Mark. *He speaks over them trying to blank it out.*

Mark   Sometimes, I just don't care about you and your wars,
                Sometimes I just don't care about you and the price of your food,
                Sometimes I just want to beat the pain up
                And kill the pressure,
                Sometimes I just want to go and scream in church
                Then fly home to make my very own Dad.

Dad   You better know your place right
                You better have manners. (*slap*)
                When I tell you to do something, you do it.
                When I say move, you move. (*slap*)

Mark   Sometimes I just don't care about you and your money.
                Sometimes I just don't care about you and your nice trainers

Scene Nine

And your nice mobile phones, with your nice holders and your nice covers.

Yes, that's right guy,

Sometimes I just don't care about your English and your Maths

And your present and your past,

Your Henry the Eighth, and your homework,

Sometimes I just don't care about you.

Sometimes I tell lies.

The truth is I care about everything, I love you Maria Shah,

But tonight, school is so unimportant,

And everything seems so loveless.

DAD *is now standing over* MOM.

DAD Yes, now you know, don't try big up yourself with me, I will damage you, you will get knock down quick. Look at me a big working man, in me own home, all I want is some service, a little tea, and you have to mek such a big ting out of it. You must know now that you can't disobey me, you must know now that I will not stand for any of your backchat. You know now ain't it, you know now ain't it? (*pause*) Now get me some tea.

MOM No.

DAD You living dangerously… I said, get me some tea.

MOM No way, I'm no slave you know.

DAD Right. (*slap*) … now what you saying?

MOM You will burn in hell, that's what I'm saying, as there is a God in heaven, you will burn in hell.

DAD *takes a pillow and smothers her face.*

Scene Nine

MARK   Oh no, not again… (*crying*) … he keeps suffocating her or something, listen, she can't breathe, sounds like he's strangling her… why does he keep doing it to her.

Click. Lights fade.

Good night.

Scene Ten

THURSDAY
WALI *at platform/pulpit.*

WALI On the fourth day, Mark did sixty press-ups, sixty squats, sixty jumping jacks, sixty sit-ups and loads of running on the spot and his fitness increaseth greatly. And on that day many leg stretches were done and quick and supple limbs were created. And Mark looked, and behold, before him he saw an Aston Villa player of the future, a goal scorer of the highest order, poetry in motion, and he thought that that was wicked.

MARK *is in his room, reading.*

MARK In this house that's falling down
We have two rooms,
One for us and one for the big people.
But the damp does not obey the rules
The damp lives in both rooms.

The damp hangs around the bathroom
Lingers in the kitchen
And watches over us like a dark menacing cloud
Waiting to explode.
The damp hugs this house; it seems to love this house.

This house is falling down
But it's still standing,
It has six rooms, three families
Two kitchens, one bathroom
And a garden that has outgrown
And disowned it.

Scene Ten

      Ants live here (I believe they speak)
      Mice live here (I believe they speak)
      Woodlice dine here (They speak with their mouths full)
      But the damp expands silently
      A shapeless body
      A cold reminder of the outside.
      I would love it if the wallpaper stayed on the walls,
      I would love to know that no more plaster
      Would fall upon my head or my bed.
      But this is it,
      The damp was here when we moved in
      And it may still be here when this house is all over.
      So don't knock it,
      This house that's falling down
      Is called my home.

Pause.

      Last night was horrible, must have been the worst night ever, I want it to stop guy, I really want it to stop, but I just hope that we don't have to run away again, I hate it when we run away, we shouldn't have to run. The thing is I like Birmingham, I like Aston, it's alright and they may not let me back into the school again. One time we ran away and we went to London and I hated it – so many people. The buses are packed, the trains are packed, even the schools are packed… no guy, I like it here, and it's so hard to mek friends there.

Scene Eleven

Mark and Wali are kicking a football around on the streets.

Mark   Run to it.

Wali   Nice one, here you are, trap this and put it on me head.

Mark   Yes, look at that for a wicked pass.

Wali   Not bad. Now watch me, watch how many kick-ups I can do. One, two, three, four, five, six.

Mark   Not bad, but Wali I think one of them touched the ground.

Wali   Oh, you put me off, I was going for twenty. OK, I tell you what, let's do some headers.

Mark   OK.

Wali   I'll count… one, two, three, four, five, six. Mark man, we didn't even get to ten, you could have got that.

Mark   Sorry guy, I wasn't concentrating.

Wali   Yeah, you wasn't concentrating alright, that was an easy ball, anyone could have got that.

Mark   Alright, alright, don't rub it in.

They start to walk away.

Wali   You'll have to do better than that on Saturday, there's gonna be some good players down there.

Mark   Yeah yeah.

Wali   So how's Maria Shah then?

Mark   I don't know.

Scene Eleven

WALI What do you mean you don't know, don't you like her any more?

MARK She's cool, her birthday's coming up or something... I don't know, I just got other things to think about now innit.

WALI What things, you worried about football trials?

MARK Football trials are no problem guy, I just hope we ain't going away again.

WALI Don't tell me that you're going to move away again?

MARK I don't know. I don't know what's happening.

WALI Find out man.

MARK (*raising his voice slightly*) I can't find out, how do you expect me to find out?

WALI OK man, don't get angry with me, I'm supposed to be your best mate man, I'm only trying to help. I told you, if you got problems at home you can tell a teacher, tell Mr Aktar, that's what he's there for – family liaison officer or something like that, they call him. Or tell the coppers because dads have to behave as well, you know. I saw on the telly right, a programme about bad dads, and one of them went to jail.

MARK OK, OK, you told me all that before.

WALI You don't have to go away again.

MARK I know, I know…

Music. They walk away.

Scene Twelve

MARK *sits on his bed.*

MARK	Wali is me best friend, but he just don't know what's really going on. Everything would be alright if I get in that squad guy, it would be like a dream come true. I can't lose this chance. You should of seen me in school today, I played some wicked football. I'm serious, I was right on form, you should have seen me, I scored four goals and I helped set up two, so I know I can do it. (*beat*) But I wish I could practise at home. The family downstairs got that big garden to themselves but they can't use it because of the neighbours. I would use it anyway – I don't care if they call me black, I'll call them white. A garden would be so cool guy. I hate this house. Mom said that one day we'll live in a whole house instead of a silly little flat and we'll have our own bathroom. Carlton won't have to sleep with Mom and Dad, and I won't have to sleep in the same room as a girl. I want a garden guy, to practise me skills. (*beat*) And guess what? Maria Shah said that I can go to her birthday party next week. She hasn't even invited Wali, only me. And I was told that most of the kids there will be girls, only a few special boys are going and I'm one of them. Well, she keeps asking me to read poems to her innit? 'Cause I mek her laugh all the time. She's always watching me when I'm playing football, now she wants me to go to her party, she likes me innit, yeah guy she wants me badly. She smells like baked beans but I still like her, but I ain't going to tell her that, am I? Anyway I think football's more important now. (*beat*) Me Mom, that's who I really love. I know hundreds of kids say that about their Moms and everyone thinks their Mom's special but my

Scene Twelve

Mom is. She ain't perfect. No one's perfect, but she's tough and she sticks by me, innit?

Tap on door, Mom *enters the room, which is dark.*

Mom	It's alright son, it's only me.
Mark	Turn the light on Mom.
Mom	No, leave it off for now. I can see.
Mark	Mom, what's the matter, are you alright?
Mom	Never mind, everything will be alright so don't worry yourself.
Mark	Mom, are we going to go away again?
Mom	Angela sleeping?
Mark	Yes.
Mom	Good.
Mark	That's all she does. Mom, are we going away again or what?
Mom	Don't you worry, we will soon be gone.
Mark	No Mom, no, we can't go… what about me football trials? I can't miss them, this is me chance to show off me skills, this is me chance to actually play at Villa Park, I can't miss that Mom… we can't go, where we going anyway?
Mom	Don't worry… (*kiss*) … it's him, he will soon be gone.

She leaves.

Mark (*to audience*) Did you see my Mom's face? Did you see it? Even in the dark I could see… You could see it, all puffed up with loads of bruises… It's the worst guy, I feel bad, I feel angry guy. I hate me Dad. He thinks he's good because he goes to work and his boss

Scene Twelve

likes him, and in church all the people say, 'Brother Campbell, you preach so good.' But you see my Mom's face, that ain't done by a good person. It's people like me Dad who give God a bad name. (*beat*) Angela wet the bed last night. It's a good job we got different beds now.

Lights fade.

Scene Thirteen

FRIDAY
Wali *at the platform/pulpit.*

WALI   On the fifth day, Mark did even more press-ups, and even more squats, jumping jacks, sit-ups and running on the spot. And his six-pack shone in all its muscular glory, and his upper body strength was tops, and he looked and he smiled for he knew that he had created a bad footballing machine, capable of two hat-tricks in ninety minutes. All was good, it was brilliant I say unto thee, he was up for it, he felt well nice. Then he said unto himself...

Light on Mark, *in his room.*

MARK   (*shouts*) Go forth and score. (*speaking quickly – excited as he shows off his books*) Yes. Wicked. Check this out, this one's poetry, and this one's football. This one's called *Oh My Word* and it's lots of short poems and raps by different poets. Fun poems you know, word play and stuff like that. And this one, well it's easy ain't it? *The Complete Encyclopaedia of Aston Villa*. Brilliant or what? I said I would do it and now this is serious, I'm gonna start me own little library. Mom said if I look after these I could get more when she can afford it. Not bad hey? And I wasn't even expecting anything. This is what happened right.
We were coming from school, Mom was doing her shopping, Carlton was in his pushchair, Angela was there, talking, talking, talking. Then we stopped to buy some vegetables and then after that I saw right in front of me, in the window of a bookshop, this book, the poetry one. Because I got it from the library before I knew it was really funny so I said to me Mom that

Scene Thirteen

one day I'll get me own copy of that. Then we went into the bookshop and we started just looking around and Mom saw this book she liked about Jamaica, and then I saw this big Villa book. So I started looking at the pictures and me Mom came up to me and said do I really want a book to take home, and I said yes, and she said which one and I said, 'Boy it's so hard to choose.' Then she went away, in a corner like, and I saw her looking in her purse and counting all her money and then, guess what? She came back and said I could have both, I couldn't believe it guy, both of them. And then guess what? She bought a book about horses for Angela, and she bought that book about Jamaica for herself. Look at that man, I can't believe it, brand new, don't mess, and I don't even have to take it back to the library. (*beat*) You wait, it's gonna happen, guy. One day you'll see me in the paper, Mark Anthony Campbell, footballer and poet, so watch out. I ain't showing off or anything, I just know what I know. Me poems are gonna make people laugh and cry, they're gonna be like intelligent poems that make people think about things going on in the world. And maybe I'll get meself a big house like Aston Hall, you know those types of houses that have a long drive and a garden like a park, that kind of house. And if I get married, I might marry a poet, yes guy, a poet wife for a poet husband... I wonder if Maria Shah is really a poet. Anyway check this out, I had this idea right, we could even have a poet priest to marry us, so he could say something like:

'Do you take this poet as your lawful wedded wife?
Do you want to live with her for all your life?
She's cool and she's wicked and she's standing at your side,
So do it poet, drop a rhyme and kiss your lovely bride.'

Scene Thirteen

(*slowing down the pace*) But I tell you what, I wouldn't hit her. I wouldn't marry someone and then beat them up, what's that for? Why marry someone and then spend so much time beating them up? If I really get upset and lose me temper, I'll just go for a walk or write a poem. I'd just say, 'We must talk dis ting over Maria,' and then we would talk about it, you know what I mean? If Angela had a husband and he hit her I would fight him but that's different ain't it? That's helping Angela, defending me sister but I ain't gonna be no wife-beater.

MARK *walks into his parents' room.*

MARK Hey Dad, look at me book, it's all about Aston Villa, it ain't half good.

DAD Yes.

MARK Do you wanna have a look?

DAD No.

MARK I got another one here – poems.

DAD Where did you get them from?

MARK Mom bought them for us today, in town. Do ya wanna have a look?

DAD No. Go to your bedroom.

MARK Dad, if you like, we can share them, me and you.

DAD I said go to your bedroom, now.

MARK *goes back to his room.*

MOM (*playing with baby Carlton*) How come you so pretty, boy? How come you so handsome? You already have all the little baby girls after you. Everybody loves my baby, everybody wants to hug my baby.

DAD (*interrupting*) Where did you get money from to waste on them books?

Scene Thirteen

Mom   I got the money from me purse, innit.

Dad   What do you mean, money in your purse? What money in your purse? Where did it come from?

Mom   What kind of stupid question is that? It's me spending money, money from my purse.

Dad   Since when have you had spending money? The money I give you, is money for food and housekeeping – I never give you money to buy books. We send kids to school to read books. Make the government buy them books, make the education people give them books, the government take plenty tax money from me for books. Right now I'm working hard to put food on the table and to pay rent, and you want buy books. Tell me, how much money have you spend on that book rubbish?

Mom   Never you mind how much.

Dad   I said tell me how much!

Mom   And I said never you mind how much.

Dad   (*really shouting*) Listen bitch, I work damn hard for you and these kids, that bloody warehouse has put me in hospital, money don't come easy, so you tell me how much of my money have you spent on stupid, ungodly books.

Mom   (*shouting*) Twenty-five pounds.

Dad   (*shouting*) Twenty-five pounds.

Mom   (*shouting*) What – you deaf? I said, twenty-five pounds.

He slaps her. She screams.

Dad   Who the hell told you to spend twenty-five quid on rubbish when we don't even have money to pay the electric bill right now? What do you think I'm made of – money?

Scene Thirteen

He slaps her. She screams.

DAD   Take those books back. Take the stupid things back and get the money back... I'll show you how to spend it.

MOM   (*screaming hysterically*) I not taking nothing back. Leave me alone. Get your hands off me, you nasty dog, move, leave me alone. Who do you think you are? Who the hell do you think you are?

DAD   I know who I am, I run tings. I pay for everything in this house. Me? I'm the man.

MOM   So what kind of man are you? What kind of man likes to hit women in their face? I'm warning you, if you touch me again I will hit you back, I ain't scared of you.

DAD   Alright, come bitch. (*slap*)

MOM   There. (*She hits him.*)

DAD   I told you, the next time you try fight me back... gonna beat you so hard, your own mother wouldn't recognise you. (*slap*)

MOM   (*loud scream*) Leave me alone... (*shouting and fighting*) Leave me alone. Who do you think you are?

DAD   I tell you, and this time I gonna teach you a lesson for good... (*slap*) You're a tramp... (*slap*) You think me, a grown man can take backchat from you? (*slap*) You think you can just spend my money as you please? (*slap*) Don't you know that if a man can't control his woman he's not a – (*slap*) man. (*slap*) So this is me, in control. (*slap, slap, slap, slap, slap, slap*)

MOM   You won't get away with this, as there is a God up in heaven, you will not get away with this.

Sound of fighting back and baby crying. MARK *is in his room, reading.*

Scene Thirteen

MARK Soon we will live quite happily
Me and my little family,
Yes soon this house that we call home
Will sigh in sweet relief.
The bad vibrations will be gone.
And joy and love will know my Mom,
And all that noise that we have known
Will just melt into peace.
My books will sit upon their shelves
All getting to know themselves,
And Angela and Carlton
Will be very young and free.
Yes, peace will come and stay with us
And surely there will be no fuss,
A house where people do not cuss?
But where will Daddy be?

Click. Lights fade.

Good night.

Scene Fourteen

SATURDAY
WALI *is at the platform/pulpit.* MARK *is in the wardrobe.*

WALI　　　　And on the sixth day everything got messed up. Wickedness happened. That's about it really, it's not good, I tell ya.

MARK　　　　No football, no bloody football. All that training for nothing. All that hard work for nothing. (*beat*)

I don't care about me Dad. Last night when he was hitting me Mom I wanted to stop him, I wanted to fight him, I wanted to do him in. I was fed up of hearing me Mom crying. I told Angela to get in here with me. So we both sat here, and we put these trousers and dresses and blankets over our heads so that we couldn't hear what was going on, but we could still hear it, it was horrible guy. We could hear Carlton crying his eyes out. You wouldn't like it, none of you would like it. And last night I had a horrible dream as well – a nightmare kind of dream. I dreamt that fighting was everywhere. People were fighting in the house; the people in the downstairs flat were fighting, when I looked outside all the people in the streets were fighting. It was like the whole world had gone to war. But not with guns, just hands, slapping and punching each other. People fighting everywhere, and all love poems or anything that was good was being burnt. We're all messed up guy, that's what can happen when you listen to your parents fighting all the time. And look now, no football, and police all over the house, just 'cause of him. I ain't coming out of here, they'll have to come and get me, this wardrobe is the safest place in this house, those adults better sort themselves

Scene Fourteen

out. (*beat*) I'll tell you something, me Dad could have been a good Dad but he didn't think... he thought about his food, his sleep, his work, and his this, that and the other, but he didn't think about us. I tried to love him but he didn't have no time for me. You know something, he never ever read one of me poems, not one, and he never ever watch me play football. He never loved me, so why should I love him? He made me Mom frightened and terrified all the time, yeah, that's real terrorism. (*beat*)

I know that not all men are like him, and I don't want to be anything like him when I grow up. (*beat*)

That's why I've got to keep writing me poetry and playing football, 'cause I wanna be the best ever, I wanna be like a legendary footballing poet, famous for scoring boss goals and doing good things. When they write the book of *The History of Aston Villa*; I wanna be in it. (*beat*) My Dad, he just couldn't stop hitting me Mom and treating her horrible. It's like this, right – me Dad didn't care about us, he didn't care about us kids, and he didn't care about me Mom.

Pause.

That's why me Mom... killed me Dad.

Lights fade to black.

Activities

Before you study the play
Independent research
Before you study the play, it would be helpful to know some background information about the author, Benjamin Zephaniah.
1. In pairs, devise a series of 15 questions about Benjamin Zephaniah. List them in a table like the one below.
2. Identify any links between your questions and order them so that they follow on logically from each other. Try to divide your questions into two or three main sections, such as 'Benjamin Zephaniah's life' and 'Benjamin Zephaniah's writing'.
3. Use the internet or your library to help you find the information you need to answer your questions. Remember to list your sources of information, as in the example below.

Question	Answer	Source
1 Where was Benjamin Zephaniah born?	Handsworth, Birmingham	Wikipedia
2 What other things has he written?		

While you are studying the play
Writing to imagine, explore and entertain
The play begins with a simple monologue from Mark, explaining his excitement about being scouted for Aston Villa. Monologues are often used in plays to share a character's feelings about an event or situation with the audience, or as an account of events, as in this case.
1. In this monologue the writer has used dialect grammar, such as *brilliant* and *innit*. Work through the monologue and identify what other techniques the writer has used to make it clear that the speaker is a teenager and that he is from Birmingham.

Activities

2. Write a monologue that describes a real or imaginary event in your life, which could be used as the opening of a play about you. When you write, use your own dialect phrases. Try to share some of your enthusiasm for the event, as Mark does in his monologue.
3. Practise reading your monologue, learning it by heart if possible so that you can perform it unaided. Think carefully about the pace and tone that you will use. You may wish to use props, as Mark does when he pulls out the Aston Villa shirt.
4. Share your performance, either as part of a group or as a performance for your class. Remember, the aim is to ensure that the audience is engaged and interested in your account of events. You should also ensure that your dialogue sounds realistic.

Drama techniques: montage

A montage is a series of images that reflects the themes, ideas, objects or emotions connected with a situation or event. Creating a montage of images and words that represents what a situation means to a character can help you to develop your understanding of the character and what might be going through their mind when faced with a situation.

1. Working with a partner and using a large sheet of paper, create a montage of images and words that represents the thoughts that Mark has as he recites the poem about Jamaica in Scene 1. For instance, it might include an image of beaches, tropical fruit, reggae, the face of Bob Marley and a Jamaican flag.
2. When you have created your montage, share it with another pair, explaining the images and words you have chosen and what they mean.
3. You may also want to choose a song to use as a soundtrack. This will help the montage come to life and be heard as well as seen.

Activities

Drama techniques: scripted drama

Some theatre and film directors use a technique called 'cross-cutting' to highlight the difference between two consecutive scenes. Benjamin Zephaniah uses this technique in Scene 2, where the action moves between Mark and his parents.

1. In a group of three, decide how you would want to stage this section. Consider what you want the contrast to demonstrate and think about the effect that the writer was trying to achieve in juxtaposing these two scenes.
2. Rehearse and prepare a performance of this section. As you prepare, consider what you want the actors who are silent to be doing on the stage – you may like to consider the use of freeze frame, for example. Think about how you can use your performance area fully in order to allow Mark to move around.
3. Present your performance to the rest of the class and then watch other groups' performances.
4. Compare the different performances of the scene. What were the differences and similarities, and why?

Layers of meaning: religious language

In Scene 4, we see Mark's dad preaching in the pulpit at church. The audience now realises the significance of the religious language that has been used in the play so far.

1. Work with a partner to reread Scenes 1 to 3. Make a list of any words or phrases that sound like they have a religious meaning.
2. Consider why you think the writer has used these words. Write a statement of between 50 and 75 words as if you are Benjamin Zephaniah, starting 'I used the religious words and phrases because…'.
3. Share your statement with the rest of the group and discuss the different reasons you have identified.

Activities

Active reading strategies: establishing empathy

In order to build up an empathy with the main character, Mark, and establish his relationships with other characters, you are going to consider further what he says about his father in Scene 4.

1 Draw a thought bubble for Mark to explore what he thinks when he hears his father preaching about Sodom and Gomorrah. Add Mark's thoughts about his father to the speech bubble, explaining what he thinks and why.
2 Consider what feelings Mark experiences as he thinks about his father, adding these around the outside of the thought bubble.

Active reading strategies: understanding the writer's viewpoint

Considering what we have seen of Mark's father so far, what do you think the writer's view of him is?

1 Go back through the text up to Scene 4 and pick out five examples of things that Mark's dad says to other characters. Make a list of these phrases and then share them with a partner.
2 With your partner, make a list of the characteristics that you consider Mark's dad to have.
3 Practise speaking aloud the lines you have chosen and try to add some of Mark's dad's characteristics to the way you say the lines.
4 Share your interpretations with another pair and ask them to identify the characteristics that you have tried to make evident in your speech.

Active reading strategies: developing understanding

In Scene 8, Mark reveals to Wali that his dad hits his mum. Wali is clearly shocked.

MARK	I'm just asking you what happens when your Dad hits your Mom.
WALI	And I just told you that he doesn't.

Activities

1. Draw a speech bubble. In it, write a statement of between 25 and 50 words that Wali might want to say to Mark at this point.
2. Form a circle with other students from your class. Select one person to represent Mark; everyone else will take it in turns to take the role of Wali. Mark should walk round the circle, stopping and facing each person in the group while they read their statement to him.
3. Finally, each person in role as Wali should read their statement aloud at the same time. This gives the impression of the range and intensity of Wali's response to Mark's revelation.

Writing to inform, explain or describe

Mark clearly knows a lot about both football and poetry. In Scene 8, he explains about the history of the English football league.

1. Choose a hobby with which you are very familiar, such as skateboarding or playing rugby, that you would like to write an article about in an information magazine for teenagers.
2. Carry out some research about your hobby. You should aim to include in your article references to different websites or texts that people could go to in order to find out more about the topic. Make sure that all your information is factually accurate by checking it against your references.
3. Plan your article carefully, considering how you can use presentation and language to appeal to your audience. You will need to write as if the topic is completely unfamiliar to them.
4. Write your article. When writing to inform, explain and describe, remember that it is important to structure your writing and develop your ideas. You will need to consider how to present the information, for example by using sub-headings, and how you can use topic sentences that are then extended into full, detailed paragraphs. Consider whether to use the second person ('you') and the present tense. You also need to think about how formal the language you use should be, as the article is aimed at teenagers.

Activities

Writing to persuade, argue and advise

In Scene 9, we witness a disturbing scene of domestic violence. One step that Mark's mum could have taken in seeking support would have been to write or talk to a friend, outlining her problem and asking for advice. In this activity, you are going to express your views on a solution by writing a response.

1 Write a letter responding to the request for help in the letter below, outlining impartially what you think Mark's mum should do. Remember that you will need to use lots of modal verbs and an imperative tone. You may also wish to offer instructions in the form of advice.

Dear Sally,

I know we've not been as close recently, but things have begun to get really bad for me and I haven't felt I could share it with you. But now I really need your help! My husband has really changed and I don't know how to cope anymore. It all started when he became more and more sexist, demanding that I do everything for him. I already wash his clothes, do his ironing, cook for him and bring up our three children practically by myself. That wouldn't be so bad, but he's started to get more and more violent. Yesterday, he hit me so hard it woke up our youngest child. I don't know what to do anymore. I wish I could walk out, but I have nowhere to go. All my friends are members of the church we go to and they would never believe my husband is a violent man. I have no friends and family I can go to here. Also, as I don't work, I've no way of saving money to leave him. He gives me everything I need for the children. I could never leave without taking the children with me, either.

I know I have to do something, but I don't know what. Please help!

Activities

Active reading strategies: predicting outcomes

Making predictions is a key way of engaging with a text. Before you read on, stop at the account of the beating at the end of Scene 9.

1. Work with a partner to make a prediction about what will happen next. You will need to use speculative language, such as *possibly, probably, perhaps* and *maybe*, to help you extend your thinking. You should also justify your predictions by explaining why you have made them.
2. Share your predictions with the rest of the class and identify any similarities.

Drama techniques: freeze frame

As we come to the final revelation about what happens, Mark says that he and his sister, Angela 'sat here' and 'put these trousers and dresses and blankets over our heads so that we couldn't hear what was going on, but we could still hear it'.

1. Working as a group of four, you are going to create a freeze frame of this moment. Decide who will take the roles of each of the characters: Mom, Dad, Mark and Angela.
2. Discuss how you are going to present your ideas, so that you show the emotions and feelings of the characters during the scene. Each of you should spend five minutes creating a thought bubble summing up your character's thoughts and feelings, so that you can try to convey these through your facial expressions, body language and use of space.
3. As a group, create your freeze frame. Make sure you consider your use of space on the stage. You should not only consider the space between you, but also how you can use the characters' positions to enhance their power. Consider who has the least power in the scene and who has the most – how can you use space to represent this visually?

Activities

Drama techniques: mime

The final line of the play is unexpected and will have a big impact on the audience.

1. Look back at the predictions that you made after the account of the beating. Compare your predictions with what actually happens.
2. With a partner, discuss how and why Benjamin Zephaniah builds up clues that misdirect the audience about what the ending will be.
3. Join up with another pair to rehearse and perform the final scene as a mime, ending with the only spoken line: 'that's why me Mom… killed me Dad.' Think about how you can make the most of the pause built into the line for dramatic effect.
4. Share your mime with the rest of the class and also watch other groups' interpretations of the final scene. Consider which mime had the most powerful impact, thinking about why this was the case. Identify what it was that the group did and comment on why their mime was so effective.

After you have studied the play

Drama techniques: freeze frame

1. Working in a group of four, discuss what you think are the three most significant events in the play.
2. For each event, select the moment in the scene that you want to freeze frame in order to explore it in more detail.
3. Prepare your three freeze frames. Consider how you will move from one freeze frame to the next.
4. Perform your sequence of freeze frames for the rest of the class. Ask the class if they know which three events you were representing. If they are not able to guess what the scenes were, ask for feedback about how you could improve your freeze frames.

Activities

5 When all the freeze frames have been performed, discuss the events that you selected. Were some more common than others? Explore why these scenes stood out more than the rest for you.

Layers of meaning: play title

1 Consider the title, *Listen to your Parents*. Think about what Benjamin Zephaniah wanted the reader to think the title meant. What did he want the reader to think it meant before reading the play? What new meanings might he have intended the reader to make by the end?

2 Draw a speech bubble like the one below. Write as if you are Benjamin Zephaniah and explain what you wanted the reader to think at the beginning of the play, and why, and then what you wanted the reader to think by the end, and why. You may be able to think of more than one thing that he might have wanted us to think.

> At the beginning, I wanted you to think that the title meant... because...
>
> By the end, I wanted you to think the title could also mean... because...

Drama techniques: conscience corridor

The relationship between Mark and his mum is not explored in much detail in this play. While the play ends dramatically, Mark's thoughts about what his mother has done are left unexpressed. A conscience corridor is a way of understanding a character's thoughts and feelings when they are faced with a critical event in the text. You are going to use a conscience corridor to explore Mark's feelings at the end of the play.

1 Prepare for this activity by considering what Mark might want to say to his mum at this moment.

Activities

2 One student should represent the character of Mark. Everyone else should form a 'corridor' down which he must walk. The diagram below shows how you need to arrange yourselves.

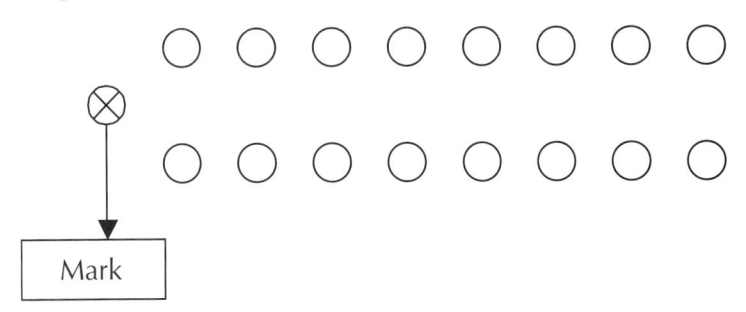

3 The student in the role of Mark should walk from one end of the corridor to the other, stopping at each person on each side on the way. Each person he stops by should say what Mark is thinking, such as 'What was the final thing that drove you to it?' or 'I forgive you, mum!'.

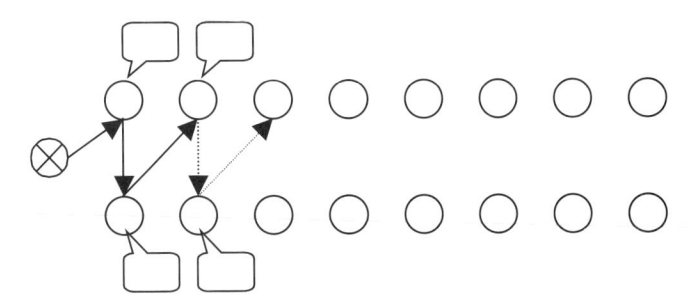

Writing a narrative commentary

Focus on the events of the play up to and including Scene 13 and think about what Wali knows about Mark's homelife. Wali sees much of what is going on in Mark's life, although we never really get to hear his side of events.

1 Write a narrative commentary, in the form of a first-person dramatic monologue, recounting the events as if you are

Activities

Wali. You should describe your thoughts and feelings, as well as giving information, because you are writing a first-person narrative. You may also wish to give a sense of atmosphere and mood to the account.

2 Try to use the following features:
- personal pronouns to show who is speaking and about whom
- temporal connectives to show the passage of time, e.g. then and next, although you may wish to think of some more advanced examples to start your sentences and direct the narrative
- a realistic 'voice' – try to use the kind of language that Mark's best friend would use to make the narrative sound genuine and to establish a sense of character.

Drama techniques: overheard conversation

One way of understanding a drama is to consider what other groups of people might say about a situation. You can use a technique called 'overheard conversation' to reflect on what other groups of people might think about the final revelation.

1 You are going to create a short improvised piece of drama that reflects the views of a group of outsiders. With a partner, decide who will appear in your improvisation: either two neighbours who have overheard many of the arguments, two members of the church congregation or two students talking in the school playground.

2 Create a short improvisation of between 30 seconds and two minutes in duration, in which you share your characters' interpretations of the murder as a piece of gossip.

3 When everyone has prepared their improvisations, your teacher will select one person to represent Mark, who should sit in the middle of the room. The pairs should stand around him and take it in turns to run through their improvisation, giving an impression of the kind of conversations Mark would be overhearing.

Activities

4 Finally, the student who took the role of Mark should speak out about what he has heard in the form of a short improvised monologue.

Wider reading

Benjamin Zephaniah has written many books for teenagers, including *Refugee Boy*, *Gangsta Rap* and *Face*. When you have finished studying *Listen to your Parents*, you might want to read one of the novels and compare it with *Listen to your Parents*.

1 Make a list of the similarities and differences between the two stories, including the following aspects.

Narrative viewpoint	Main character	Families
Who is telling the story? What similarities are there between the two texts?	What similarities and differences are there between the main characters?	What similarities and differences are there between the families?
Tone	**Themes**	**Issues**
What similarities and differences are there in the narrative voices that the writer uses?	What are the two texts about and what similarities and differences are there between them?	What are the main problems in the two texts and how do these compare?
Written style	**Audience**	**Your response**
What similarities and differences are there between the way the two texts are written?	Who do you think would enjoy each of the stories? What similarities and differences are there between the intended audiences of the two texts?	Which did you prefer, and why?

Activities

Writing to analyse, review and comment

Following your comparison of the two Benjamin Zephaniah texts, you are going to write a short analysis commenting on them and explaining what they do that is similar and what they do differently.

1 Your writing should provide a balanced analysis, so you will need to make sure you use paragraphs that connect the two analyses with connectives of comparison and contrast. Before you start writing, make a list of comparative and contrasting connectives, such as *similarly* and *on the other hand*. Try to make sure you have at least five or six different connectives for comparing and five or six for contrasting, so that you can use them to help you structure your writing.

2 Write your analysis. Make sure you use the appropriate connectives to help you structure your writing and that you also use evidence from the two texts. It will be particularly helpful if you revisit your notes from the previous activity and add details of examples from the text that support your view.

Reading for pleasure

If you enjoyed reading *Listen to your Parents*, why not try…

You Don't Know Me by David Klass

John is fourteen years old, alienated and angry. His mother's boyfriend is using him as a punch bag and his teachers don't understand him at all. Feeling completely alone, John retreats into his imagination. Only through his humorous take on life and his escapist fantasies can you begin to know him …

ISBN 978 0 582 77758 3

The Drowning Pond by Catherine Forde

A realistic insight into female gang culture. Nicky longs to be one of the beautiful crowd at school, so when Bella invites her into her inner circle, she is overjoyed. But the truth is, Bella is only interested in Nicky's gorgeous brother, Luke. When Bella and her gang tire of Nicky, she hatches a plan to gang up on the weird new girl and convince the others that she's a witch … but how far will they go?

ISBN 978 1 4058 2849 9

Reading for pleasure

The Outsiders by S. E. Hinton

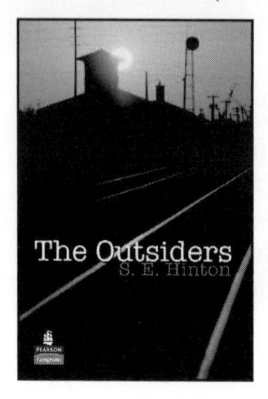

A gritty modern American classic, written when the author was only 17. According to Ponyboy, you're either a Greaser or a Soc. Coming from the wrong side of town, he's a Greaser and his high school rivals are the Socs – the kids who have the money, the attitude and can get away with anything. The Socs love to spend their time beating up the Greasers, but Ponyboy and his friends know what to expect and stick together. But one night someone goes too far, and Ponyboy's world begins to crumble.

ISBN 978 1 4058 6395 7